This *JAMARI* book belongs in the saddle of:

_____

Grains of Wisdom

A COLLECTION OF ILLUSTRATED PROVERBS

Belinda É. S.

First Published in 2015 by Samari Publishing Ltd.

ᒍᐱᐱᒪᐱᒥ

P u b l i s h i n g

www.samaripublishing.com
contact@samaripublishing.com

Illustrations by Hajdi S. Adamovic
Watercolours by Berta Jimenez Martinez
Translations by Lily Kahn

Printed in Serbia by Euro Dream
Digitised by the Creative Media Services team at University College London
The font used is Caslon Antique copyright of Alan Carr (1998), originally designed by Bernard William "Berne" Nadal in 1895

ISBN: 978-0-9935010-0-5

for every open heart willing to hear

Hajdi, your illustrations are gorgeous, this book wouldn't have been the same without you.
Berta, your beautiful brush strokes made these pictures come alive.
Lily, thank you so much for your discerning translations, I'm so glad you could be a part of this.
Raheel Nabi / Mary Hinkley / Alejandro Lopez - thank you for making these illustrations shine in their digital format.
I am grateful for your help and expertise.
Mom & Dad - thanks for lovingly nurturing the gift of creativity and the arts, you let me dream and gave me space to create.
And thanks for passing on your own grains of wisdom.
God, thanks for creativity and inspiration.
And last but not least, Gogi, thanks for being my support
and the witness to all my creative madness.

thank you

Dear Readers,

Once long ago there lived a man whose name was Solomon. He was a very wise king so one day King Solomon began to write down wise proverbs - little bits of advice that a person could easily remember. These proverbs could help people if they ever got stuck and needed guidance. It's a good thing he wrote them down because now, thousands of years later, people like you and me can read them (in a book called the Bible) and find some good advice for our own lives!

This book is a collection of some of my favourite proverbs along with some beautiful illustrations. I hope you enjoy looking at them, thinking about the wise sayings and I also hope you have fun putting them into practice! Always remember, when you're not sure what to do and you find yourself in a sticky situation, come back to this book, leaf through and I'm sure you'll find something to help you.

-- Belinda

* For you readers with little ones, I've envisioned that you would read this book with them, perhaps cuddled up at the end of the day or whilst travelling, to use the illustrations and proverbs as a springboard into conversations that will help them grasp the meaning of the sayings and especially how they can apply them in their day-to-day life. I hope you find that spending time with Grains of Wisdom will be an enriching experience for you and your family. Happy reading!

Drawn-out hope makes the heart sick...

but when a desire is fulfilled, it is a tree of life. 13:12

Singing songs to a person with a heavy heart is like
taking away their clothes on a cold day or pouring vinegar on a wound. 25:20

People who go around gossiping tell secrets,
but trustworthy people keep them to themselves. 11:13

Advice in someone's heart is like deep water,
but a person of understanding can draw it out. 20:5

Just as water reflects a face, so a person's heart reflects the person. 27:19

A portion of vegetables served with love

is better than a fattened ox served with hate. 15:17

Lazy people don't even roast the game they've hunted,
but to diligent people resources are precious. 12:27

Plan all of your work outside and prepare it in the
field before you build your house. 24:27

The name of the Eternal One is a tower of strength;
the righteous run into it and are safe. 18:10

It's not good to eat too much honey or to seek out glory for yourself. 25:27

If you dig a pit-trap...

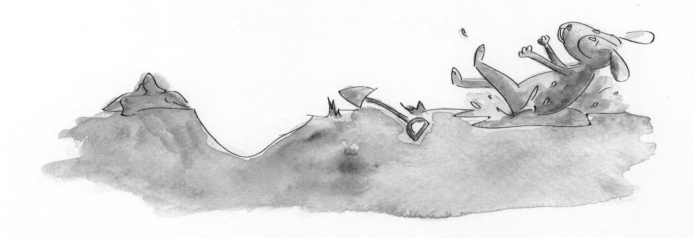

you'll fall into it yourself. 26:2

Starting an argument is like opening a floodgate,

so stop before the disagreement breaks out. 17:14

Don't withhold good things from those who deserve them,

if it's in your power to do so. 3:27

The words of gossipers are like sweets; they sink deep into the belly. 18:8

A joyful heart is good medicine, but a broken spirit dries out the bones. 17:22

Someone with no control over their moods is like
a broken-down city without walls. 25:28

The heart of a wise person seeks knowledge,
but the mouth of a fool grazes on nonsense. 15:14

People who have isolated themselves seek
their own desire; they argue with all good advice. 18:1

Listen to your father, who brought you into the world,
and don't show contempt for your mother when she gets old. 23:22

A hot-tempered person starts arguments,

while a patient person quiets down quarrels. 15:18

People who cover their ears against the cries of the poor

will not be answered when they themselves cry out. 21:13

When there's no wood fires go out, and when there's no gossip arguments stop. 26:20

Those who love the pure of heart and speak with grace
will have a king as their friend. 22:11

Relying on an untrustworthy person in a time of need is like
relying on a bad tooth or a wobbly foot. 25:19

If your enemies are hungry, feed them; if they are thirsty,
give them water to drink. 25:10

People who hide their sins will not prosper,

but people who confess and leave them behind will be given mercy. 28:13

Fools show their anger immediately...

but clever people ignore insults. 12:16

A friend loves at all times...

and a brother is born to help in times of trouble. 17:7

{the end}

BELINDA is a psychologist who specialises in Expressive Arts Therapy with an MA in Hebrew and Jewish Studies. She is also a musician and composer, working towards a PhD in Ancient Greek Philosophy. [Belinda likes dark chocolate, and the sound when swimming underwater.]

HAJDI is a freelance designer and illustrator. She has experience in desktop publishing, music album covers, and marketing literature. Hajdi is also a qualified Interior Designer and a mother of two. [As a child, Hajdi used to make cakes out of mud and bring home unwanted puppies and kittens.]

BERTA is a Spanish painter artist. Her main work consists of oils, pastels, acrylics and watercolors. She has extensive experience in painting exhibitions in Spain. Berta is also an illustrator of books and records. [When Berta was a little girl she used to think that animals understood her when she talked to them; now she's sure they do!]

LILY completed her BA , MA , & PhD in the Department of Hebrew and Jewish Studies at University College London, specialising in Hebrew and Yiddish philology. She teaches Biblical Hebrew, Rabbinic Hebrew, Ugaritic and the Yiddish language. [Lily was named after the last queen of Hawaii and has two dogs, Tails and Panda.]

belinda é. s